To Dean Austin, the man I'm happy to have rule over
me. I reach for his hand; it's always there.

Woman's Divine Destiny

Woman's Divine Destiny

Mildred Chandler Austin

Deseret Book Company   Salt Lake City, Utah   1980

Library of Congress Cataloging in Publication Data

Austin, Mildred Chandler, 1926-
  Woman's divine destiny.

  Includes index.
  1. Woman (Mormonism) I. Title.
BX8641.A9   261.8'34'12   78-21274
ISBN 0-87747-733-7

Acknowledgments

The quotations in this book come from a much larger compilation; for my master's thesis at Brigham Young University I collected many of the words presidents of The Church of Jesus Christ of Latter-day Saints have said to, for, and about women. It isn't necessary to include them all here, for they have been consistently the same, ever since the days of Adam and Eve. The statements in this compilation are representative of many more.

Even though these truths have been expounded through the years, they weren't publicized as much as I needed them to be. How I wish I had known them more thoroughly when I was a bride. How grateful I am to have finally learned and incorporated them into my life-style. They work! My motivation in sharing them is the hope that they will help today's young wives and mothers to raise the sanctified generation the Doctrine and Covenants tells us we must have in order to build the New Jerusalem. (105:31.)

Dr. Richard O. Cowan and Dr. Robert C. Patch supervised the thesis work, parent to this one. I greatly appreciate their help, along with the encouragement and writing assistance of Virginia DeHart. Dr. James W. Fitch and Dr. Gordon Mauss gave me the opportunity to teach the institute of religion classes that resulted in this writing. Their faith in me and the willingness of Latter-day Saint women in the Los Angeles area to accept the words of the prophets in place of the theories of men gave me the courage I needed. I'm grateful to them all.

My greatest gratitude, however, is to my mother, Mrs. William James Chandler, whose artistry in playing the roles of wife and mother taught me how to perform. Besides offering that example, she instilled in me a desire to find complete fulfillment by studying the precepts the Lord has so graciously given us on the subject.

Contents

Introduction

A number of years ago, as an early morning seminary teacher, I heard the Salt Lake area supervisors tell us our job was to convince our students that the answers to their problems can be found in the scriptures. I didn't know this for myself, but I took their word for it and passed it on to my students.

During the course of my work at Brigham Young University as I earned my master's degree in Mormon doctrine, I gained a personal testimony that what the seminary supervisors had told us was and is true: the answers to our questions really can be found in the scriptures, ancient and modern. God's spokesmen, the prophets, have given us ample direction for every facet of our lives. The Lord has given us very clear guidelines to follow, and then has invited us to ask him for more personal direction. If we stumble because of a lack of information, it is only because we haven't turned on the light—gospel light. Extra light for our specific problems is available to us; the switch is pressed by the bended knee.

We mustn't be like the farmer who, when electricity had just become available for domestic use, finally agreed to let his house be wired for power. As a selling point, the salesman told him that with electric power, the house could be as light at midnight as it was at noon. So the contract was signed and the wiring job was done.

Some time later the salesman was riding around the

area after dark and noticed that the light from the farmer's windows was no brighter than it had been when he had been using kerosene lamps. Being an honorable man, the salesman decided to investigate. After being greeted caustically, he asked to be allowed to try to find the problem. He knew that a reliable electrician had done the wiring and had installed cable for carrying high voltage, so he looked first at the light bulbs being used. Sure enough, they were the problem. They were ten-watt bulbs.

People often make a similar mistake in their own lives. We all come to earth "wired" for great light—the Light of Christ. "And the Spirit giveth light to every man that cometh into the world. . . ." (D&C 84:46.) When we receive the gift of the Holy Ghost, we receive the capacity to receive greater light, while receiving the priesthood gives the recipient the ability to receive even more light. We're more foolish than the farmer in the story if we use only a fraction of the wattage available to us.

In order to make full use of our gospel light we need to do two things. First, we must study and believe the words of the prophets, God's spokesmen. The Savior tells us that we should receive the prophet's word "as if from mine own mouth, in all patience and faith." (D&C 21:5.) Second, when we have studied what God has given as general guidelines, if our personal questions are still unanswered in full, we can receive additional light by adhering to the direction given in such scriptures as 1 Nephi 11:1, 2 Nephi 32:3-4, Enos 1:10, and Doctrine and Covenants 8:2 and 9:9.

The specific information that interested me in my graduate work concerned what the Lord expects of his daughters, and what is his definition of woman's role. I spent two years compiling everything I could find that the presidents of the Church have said to, for, and about women. After this work was all done, it became obvious to me that the Lord had actually said it all at the very beginning, in the garden of Eden. All his words to women since then have served to explain or amplify his early message.

To Eve and her daughters the Lord gave some directives that still apply today. Every wife is instructed to (1) be a helpmeet to her husband; (2) let her husband rule over her; (3) be one flesh with her husband; and (4) be a mother and multiply. (See Moses 3:20-25; 4:22.)

Understanding these directives and what each involves has given me greater insight into what the Lord expects of me. With such understanding, I have been able to work more effectively at fulfilling my role as a woman and wife.

"A Comfort unto My Servant"

Turning to the original Bible language for a definition of "helpmeet" gives us a better understanding of this first directive of the Lord. In Hebrew, a helpmeet is "a helper peculiar to, appropriate to, according to one's need." So that is clear—our first calling as women is to be whatever our husbands need us to be. Now all we have to find out is what they need us to be.

For the answer to that question let's turn to the great revelation to women in the latter days—section 25 of the Doctrine and Covenants. This was given through the Prophet Joseph to his wife Emma, but the Lord states clearly, "this is my voice unto all." (V. 16.) To Emma Smith—and all wives—the Savior says, "And the office of thy calling shall be for a comfort unto my servant, . . . thy husband." (V. 5.) Here the Lord directs our thinking right back to our primary calling: our husbands. Knowing how intoxicating the applause of the world can be, God warns us to "beware of pride. Let thy soul delight in thy husband, and the glory which shall come upon him." (V. 14.) The next statement tells us why this is so important: it's the only way we can hope to someday wear a crown, be a queen in heaven. The scriptures state clearly that unless a woman's husband takes her to exaltation, she's not going.

A man can't gain great glory without his wife either. "Only through this sacred ordinance of a temple marriage can members of the Church receive an exaltation in the ce-

4

lestial kingdom." (Harold B. Lee, *Improvement Era,* June 1957, p. 407.) The husband must achieve the high plane and pull his wife up with him, but she must give him the boost he needs to achieve those heights in the first place. The boosting mechanism that is the most effective, as God told us in section 25 of the Doctrine and Covenants, is to be a comfort to one's husband.

I once heard a marriage counselor talk about how one should choose a mate as he chooses a shoe: if it isn't a good fit, it will be painful. If we consider this shoe-to-foot analogy, we can see the husband as being the foot, having to climb the rocky road to exaltation. A bare foot is going to find the path too painful; it needs a comforter, a shoe. Of course, this is where the analogy is weak—a shoe is inferior to a foot and wives are not inferior to husbands, a point we will discuss in depth later. So let's just overlook the weakness now while we consider the analogy's helpful, good points.

When I consider what makes a shoe truly comfortable, I see more clearly how to be a comforting wife. What does a comfortable shoe do for a foot? It supports but is also pliant. Good leather molds itself to the demands of the foot, whereas if the foot yields to the shoe, the foot becomes misshapen and doesn't perform as well. The shoe needs to do the yielding as it cushions the hard places. This yielding can be minimal if proper care has been given to the fitting of shoe and foot.

Those of us playing the roles of shoes need to seriously consider what happens to shoes that are painful. They are generally discarded and a more comfortable pair takes their place. Some men are honorable enough to endure the pain of uncomfortable shoes. For instance, when the men of Zion's Camp were marching to help the suffering Saints in Missouri, many of them found themselves with poor-fitting boots. The historical account tells us that the blood would drip out of their boots when they removed them at the day's end. These men were of exceptionally high caliber. But far too many pain-producing wives have learned that their husbands aren't that long-suffering, and have found out how it feels to be discarded.

When a man finds a really comfortable pair of shoes, all-purpose shoes that will carry him hiking and then shine up nicely to wear for dancing, how does he regard them? He realizes that he can't get along without them, and takes the best care of them, having them resoled as often as necessary to keep them in good shape. Wives bring happiness to themselves as well as their husbands when they heed the Lord's advice to become skillful at comforting.

A woman named Paula learned this lesson the hard way. Her husband, obviously not of Zion's Camp quality, was tired of her nagging so he moved out and started divorce proceedings. Paula hadn't meant to drive him away, because she loved him deeply, so when she heard about the importance of a wife's comforting instead of judging her husband she vowed to try. The only problem was that he wouldn't come back home to give her a chance.

Then fate stepped in. Paula heard on a newscast that her husband, a truck driver by profession, had been involved in an accident about fifty miles from her home, and that the driver of the other vehicle had been killed. When her husband didn't call on her for help, she asked her home teachers to drive her to the town where the accident had occurred and to go with her from one motel to another until she found her grieving spouse. His emotions were bruised and battered, so she cradled and soothed him until he couldn't resist going home with her. So great was her determination to win him back that she did everything she could to be a comfort to him. It wasn't long before he withdrew his divorce plans, and the last I heard from them they were still very happily married.

This one concept, comforting instead of judging, changed Paula's marriage from a ten-watt, dying union to

a brightly beaming production. A wife should never minimize the tremendous power of being a comfort unto her
husband.

Many tales in Church history show that it isn't just
"weakling husbands" who need comforting. Typical of
these is the following story:

President Wilford Woodruff's wife, Phoebe, was very ill
and died. She later told how, after leaving her body, she
followed a heavenly messenger to a place of great splendor.
There she was shown scenes from the future life of her husband, all the trauma of LDS history that was part of
President Woodruff's experience, ending with his terribly
difficult decision to issue the Manifesto. Then Phoebe was
given a choice. She could remain where she was or, if she
would be the true helpmeet her husband would need to get
him through this future, she could return to her family on
earth.

Though Phoebe thought how nice it would be to
remain in such beauty, she looked at her grieving husband
and baby and agreed to return to mortality and be the
comfort this great man needed his wife to be. In his
biography, Elder Woodruff says that he was impressed to
give her a blessing that would restore her to life. He did so,
and Phoebe was back to keep her promise. President
Woodruff's great success in mortality is an indication of
how well she played her part. (Matthias F. Cowley, *Wilford
Woodruff* [Bookcraft, 1964], p. 97.)

As a Man Thinketh

Joseph Smith told the members of the first Relief Society that one of the most effective ways a woman can comfort her husband is to place confidence in him. (*History of the Church* [HC] 4:604.) Behavioral scientists since the days of wise King Solomon have been telling us how very important the male ego is. "As [a man] thinketh in his heart, so is he." (Proverbs 23:7.) People tend to live up to the expectations of the significant others in their lives—self-fulfilling prophecy is a very real concern.

It all comes down to the fact that we often dictate the role we expect our spouse to play. Reinforcing the qualities we want to enlarge makes him grow. Marriage counselors today tell us that whatever treatment a wife is receiving, positive or negative, she is reinforcing it. So, to upgrade the behavior of one's husband, a wife needs to give him the role of the hero in the script she hands to him.

One friend of mine is living in great sorrow because she won't accept the Prophet's advice and build her husband's self-confidence, his "divine concept." Ever since their wedding day she has been telling him, "You'll never be as good a man as my father." Now she's suing for divorce because he is an alcoholic. Unaware of the harm she may have done to her husband, she thinks he is the villain in this tragedy. But he's merely playing the role she handed him.

In contrast to this sad story is the happy one of my daughter-in-law. Even before she married my son she was saying, "He's the finest man I've ever known." Such a statement made me gasp; he was a fine boy, but I had raised him and knew that he had his share of weaknesses. Besides that, I feared that such a statement would hurt her good father's feelings. Nevertheless, she has kept on saying it, and her husband is beginning to fit the part. He has matured beautifully since their marriage. It has been said that the wife finishes raising the boy, and we're grateful that our son's life is in the hands of this wise woman.

We needn't wait for modern research to verify Joseph Smith's statement that wives should place confidence in their husbands. His successor, President Brigham Young, emphasized this concept for us as well. He told wives whose husbands were not performing properly that they shouldn't let their faith in these husbands drop, but should continue to uphold them in the "dignity of their position and calling," letting them be the "head all day long." He urged wives to show wisdom by not complaining, for "a woman's wisdom and judgment has failed her once in the choice of a husband, and it may again, if she is not very careful. By seeking to cast off her husband—by withdrawing her confidence and goodwill from him, she casts a dark shade upon his path, when, by pursuing a proper course of love, obedience, and encouragement, he might attain to that perfection she had anticipated in him." (*Journal of Discourses* [JD] 7:280.)

This valuable lesson can be traced back even farther, to King Lamoni's wife in the Book of Mormon. Remember how the sons of King Mosiah, after their own conversions to the truth, wanted to take the gospel to the heathen Lamanites? Their welcome was not exactly cordial—three of them were cast into prison and persecuted terribly. The fourth missionary, Ammon, avoided such treatment by being a fine servant to King Lamoni. While doing this service Ammon performed, with the Lord's help, a miracle that made the king very receptive to his message. After hearing the gospel story the king was "carried away in the spirit" and his body fell to the earth as though it were dead. (Maybe he received a greater charge of light than his body was yet prepared to handle.) After two days and two nights of seeing him apparently dead, Lamoni's court, including his sons and daughters, urged his wife to have him buried. They pointed out to her that his body was already decaying.

Not perceiving her husband as the others did, Lamoni's wife called Ammon to her and said, "To me he doth not stink." (Alma 19:5.) Ammon, and later Lamoni, praised her for her faith and rejoiced in it. This faith, coupled with the servant girl's help in getting the multitude there, made it possible for the Lord to miraculously raise Lamoni before a great number of people, preconditioning them for conversion to the gospel. A whole nation joined the church because one woman refused to accept society's estimate of her husband.

King Lamoni's wife exemplifies the wisdom of President David O. McKay's advice that before marriage we should keep our eyes wide open, but after the ceremony we should keep them half-shut—shut to our spouse's weaknesses. (*Conference Report* [CR], April 1956, p. 9.) This is done by concentrating so fully on strengths that weaknesses get ignored.

"You young wives must realize that as your companion comes home from his day's labor, he comes sometimes with nerves that are taut with the tensions of that day's efforts, hoping to find in you someone to give him the strength and courage to go back inspired and better prepared to meet the problems of the next day. To nag and to scold and to fail to appreciate his problems is to fail in being the companion that he needs." (Harold B. Lee, *Youth and the Church* [Deseret News Press, 1945], p. 178.)

Sister Lee added to this advice from her husband, saying that when her husband performed temple marriages, "his counsel to the bride has been to stand by her husband's side, support him, be the mother of his children, and the one who gives him faith when he sometimes loses faith in himself." (*Church News,* April 3, 1971, p. 3.)

Joseph Smith told the members of the first Relief Society some important methods of expressing this confidence in their husbands. Much can be done verbally, by the things we say as well as the things we refrain from saying. He said: "When you go home, never give a cross or unkind word to your husbands, but let kindness, charity and love crown your works henceforward." (HC 5:107.) He used the word *never*—not even when the man is making a misstep should cross or unkind words be used. Even then, he said, "You need not be teazing [*sic*] your husbands because of their deeds, but let the weight of your innocence, kindness and affection be felt" because, he added, it is "more mighty."

"Not war, not jangle, not contradiction, or dispute, but meekness, love, purity—these are the things that should magnify you in the eyes of all good men." (HC 4:605.)

Brigham Young said this about teasing wives: ". . . there are men in this city . . . who are driven from this duty [praying] by the teazing [*sic*] of a wife. 'Now, pa, come, do let us have prayers; I have got all the children here and the Bible, and I do want to have prayers.' He cannot bow to that kind of compulsion, to save him; and if he should be damned he will not be made to pray in such a manner, for when he prays he means to do it for his God, and not because a woman teases him to do it. . . . I should never pray in creation, if I could not do it independent of the dictation of a woman." (JD 9:248.)

Orson Hyde remarked, concerning criticism:

I know it is sometimes the case that a person will see a chance to slip in a word that cuts like a razor. "Oh, that is too good a chance to let slip; therefore I will let fly a word," and it sets all hell on fire. . . . The woman sees a chance to give the man a keen word that will make him feel; but she sours her own dish by so doing. She turns the sweet into gall, and then is compelled to eat it.

What is the better way? If she sees a chance to inflict a wound by a word that will cut, and she thinks her husband really deserves it, which is the sure way to get a victory? Never say that word! . . . Let it pass, I tell you; take it mildly; and, by-and-by, says the husband, "I grieved my wife, and gave her just cause of offence. I am sorry for it; she has taken it so meekly, and never has harrassed my feelings. Now, this cuts me ten times worse than if she had said something to balance the matter: then I should not have had this sting in my heart. But to see her take it so mildly without offering one reproach, . . . how can I forgive myself?" When you get a victory in that way, it is worth something. (JD 6:158.)

President Joseph F. Smith repeated the warning to wives to never verbalize unkind thoughts about their husbands. He cautioned wives never to let their words be sarcastic and cutting, nor should they pass slurs and insinuations. They should never nag their husbands, he said. (CR, April 1905, pp. 84-85.) Then this prophet gave us another important method of expressing confidence in our husbands: truly putting our lives into their hands and depending upon them to handle such responsibility well. He said:

A wife may love her husband, but it is different to that of the love of mother to her child. The true mother, the mother who has the fear of God and the love of truth in her soul, would never hide from danger or evil and leave her child exposed to it. But as natural as it is for the sparks to fly upward, as natural as it is to breathe the breath of life, if there were danger coming to her child, she would step between the child and that danger; she would defend her child to the uttermost. Her life would be nothing in the balance, in comparison with the life of her child. That is the love of true motherhood—for children.

Her love for her husband would be different, for if danger should come to him, as natural as it would be for her to step between her child and danger, instead her disposition would be to step behind her husband for protection; and that is the difference between the love of mother for children and the love of wife for husband. (*Improvement Era*, May 1910, p. 277.)

Unless these words are reviewed often it is easy for a wife to fight her husband's battles. If she does this she is treating him as a child, and history shows that he will probably react as a child. The big battle I'm tempted to help my husband fight for me is the battle of the budget. I could bring in a good income, but I don't, even though having too much month left at the end of the money leaves him battered and bruised. I want to be married to a man, not a child, so I take President Smith's advice and let him fight the battle—but then I try to make it worth the fight for him. If he were hurt in a battle with a lion I would do my best to comfort the wounds and make him glad he defended me. I can and must make his battle with the budget seem worthwhile by spending the means he gives me to comfort him, to make his home a heaven to him.

Elder Boyd K. Packer has said:

It has been interesting to me that many couples who come for help—some of them with grown children—haven't the vaguest idea about some of the very basic considerations in the husband-wife relationship.

Some women, long married, have no idea, it seems, about how a man is put together, what his needs are, how he can be lifted and inspired and encouraged. . . .

Now, first one suggestion with reference to him that you may want to think about. He needs to know that he is protecting you. He needs to feel and know that he is the leader in the family.

He needs a wife and a sweetheart with whom he can share his love, with whom he can have its full, complete expression. He needs to have a circle—a family circle with children. This makes all that he must face out in the world seem worthwhile. He needs to feel dominant. He needs to be the protector.

When he feels this he is a better man. He is a better husband. He is a better employee, a better employer. He is better adjusted and happier in life. He can do better work. He can even be more prosperous. But for the sake of all that is important, above all, he can be a better father, and a better holder of the priesthood.

Young sisters, if you take that role from him, the one he needs, you reduce his manhood. (*BYU Speeches of the Year,* April 14, 1970, p. 5.)

Do all men need to have their wives expressing confidence in them? The greatest ones regularly acknowledge that they do. Sister Barbara Smith, president of the Relief Society of the Church, reported this story to me as President Spencer W. Kimball told it to her. He said that very early in his married life he was given a Church responsibility that overwhelmed him with its seeming magnitude. He said to his bride, "I can't, I can't, I can't." She answered with, "You can, you can, you can. The Lord will help you, and I will help you." Then President Kimball talked of how his Camilla has been giving him that kind of reinforcement ever since, of how much he has needed and appreciated it.

Joseph Smith acknowledged the importance of the comforting he received from Emma. He reported how one time they had a fight and he was incapable of carrying on his work until they were again living in harmony. (B. H. Roberts, *Comprehensive History of the Church*, 1:131.)

Later, when in hiding from Missouri ruffians who were still determined to destroy him, he wrote this tribute to her: ". . . with what unspeakable delight, and what transports of joy swelled my bosom, when I took by the hand, on that night, my beloved Emma—she that was . . . the wife of my youth, and the choice of my heart. Many were the reverberations of my mind when I contemplated for a moment the many scenes we had been called to pass through, the fatigues and the toils, the sorrows and sufferings, the joys and consolations from time to time, which had strewed our paths and crowned our board. Oh what a commingling of thought filled my mind for the moment, again she is here, even in the seventh trouble [seven months pregnant]—undaunted, firm, and unwavering—unchangeable, affectionate Emma!" (HC 5:107.)

Joseph Smith's mother, Lucy Mack Smith, tells us in her biography of Joseph of how she learned the great importance of confidence-building and comforting. Shortly after her marriage she became very ill, so ill that it looked as if she would surely die. Her mother, who was caring for her, left her briefly, and when she came back to the bedside she took one look and said, joyfully, "Lucy, you are better." Lucy answered, "Yes, mother, the Lord will let me live, if I am faithful to the promise which I made to him, to be a comfort to my mother, my husband, and my children." (*History of Joseph Smith by His Mother, Lucy Mack Smith* [Stevens and Wallis, 1945], p. 34.)

Woman, the Wall

O ne of the most difficult commandments for women to accept, especially in today's world, is God's directive that the husband should "rule over" his wife. President Brigham Young recognized this trial and expressed his sympathy, saying, "I do not know what the Lord could have put upon women worse that he did upon Mother Eve, where he told her: 'Thy desire shall be to thy husband.'" (JD 16:167.)

After acknowledging the difficulty, President Young offered a possible solution to it: "Says a woman of faith and knowledge, 'I will make the best of it; it is a law that man shall rule over me; his word is my law, and I must obey him; he must rule over me; this is upon me and I will submit to it,' and by so doing she has promises that others do not have." (Ibid.)

President Lorenzo Snow also recognized the difficulty women have with this challenging dictum and told how we can make it work well for us. He said: "Now, you sisters, . . . call upon the Lord, and he will give you power to obey your husbands; and do you pray that they may be able to execute the designs of the Almighty, and that the enemy may have no power over them." (JD 5:325.)

In the last general Relief Society conference in October 1975, President Spencer W. Kimball made this directive easier for women to accept. He said that the commandment meant "he shall preside over thee" instead of "he

16

shall rule over thee." This helps erase the feeling that there is a superiority factor in the husband-wife relationship. Men's and women's roles are equally important, but not identical.

One of the women of the early days of Utah wrote an analogy for the *Woman's Exponent* that makes this concept more clear. She said that in the ideal home the husband is like the foundation of a house, the wife is like the wall, and the children are like the planks of the roof, resting directly upon the wall but ultimately supported by the foundation.

Because foundations bear the burden, they must also make most of the decisions, such as where the house will be located, how large it will be, and what shape it will take. God's spokesmen, ancient and modern, have been unwavering in their proclamations that the husband is to be the decision-maker at home, the head of the house. Wives act as counselors to their husbands but are never supposed to dictate the decisions.

President Brigham Young said, "Let the father be the head of the family, the master of his own household; and let him treat them as an angel would treat them; and let the wives and children say amen to what he says, and be subject to his dictates, instead of their dictating the man, instead of their trying to govern him." (JD 4:55.)

President Young admitted that "women are more ready to do and love the right than men are" (JD 12:194), but then to self-righteous wives he gave this warning: "If that mother or wife enjoys the gift of the Holy Ghost, she will never intrude upon the rights of her husband"— neither should she dictate to him in his business. (JD 11:135.)

President Lorenzo Snow offered this advice on humility: "It is much more difficult for wives to learn than it is for husbands, because women have not the degree of light and knowledge that their husbands have." He also said that "while a man is full of the Spirit and power of the

Almighty he perceives the line of duty in a moment." (JD 5:315.)

Section 84 of the Doctrine and Covenants tells us that one of the gifts of the Melchizedek Priesthood is to know the mysteries of God. (V. 19.) I don't hold the priesthood; therefore I will never have access to as much knowledge as my husband does. Through the gift of the Holy Ghost I can use the Lord's vast library, but as a Melchizedek Priesthood holder my husband has a key to its "Special Collections Room." If I want to know what is in there for me and the rest of my family I must boost him upstairs to that level so he can retrieve the information for us.

Nephi gave wives a good example of how to boost others. (See 1 Nephi 16:18-32.) As Lehi and his family were traveling across the desert to the ocean where they could embark for the promised land, they were very much dependent upon meat for their sustenance. Therefore it was a cause of great concern as the men's bows began to break; and when Nephi's bow, their last, broke, it was a great tragedy. They saw starvation in the wilderness ahead, and all of them, including Lehi, were murmuring against the Lord—all except Nephi, that is. Instead of murmuring, he did something about their situation. He worked until he had another good bow manufactured.

Then, wives, he put the prophet right back up in the saddle the same way we should uplift our husbands when they perform poorly. He didn't usurp Lehi's role, but went to his father and asked him to go to the Lord and find out where they could go to find animals for their meat. By so doing he expressed the confidence in Lehi that helped him see himself again as a prophet. Thus encouraged and supported, Lehi resumed his prophetic role and never allowed himself to slip again.

Think what an adverse effect it would have had on Lehi if his son Nephi had bypassed him in his efforts to get the Lord's help. Sometimes husbands, the family prophets, stumble. At such times wives must be especially careful to be boosters, to lay down a sturdy support upon which the husband can climb to regain the "special collections" level of God's library, where he can again use his key to receive divine direction for the family.

This is a difficult role to play, following a struggling husband when one's sights are set on glories far afield. President Joseph F. Smith reinforced this concept with this admonition: "In the home the presiding authority is always vested in the father, and in all home affairs and family matters there is no authority paramount. . . .

"It is a question largely of law and order," he continued, "and its importance is seen from the fact that the authority remains and is respected long after a man is really unworthy to exercise it." (*Juvenile Instructor*, March 1, 1902, pp. 146-47.)

What confusion that statement can bring, because we have been told by several of our prophets that we're not expected to follow our husbands to hell (see, for example, Brigham Young, JD 8:141), but that we're to follow them in righteousness. The question, then, seems to revolve around who is to be the judge of their righteousness. Nowhere have I seen women given the prerogative of judging their husbands. Priesthood leaders, acting as our Father's representatives, are a man's judges—his wife is not. She is his comfort-giver.

This concept has been taught throughout ecclesiastical history. "Likewise, ye wives, be in subjection to your own husbands . . . Even as Sara obeyed Abraham, calling him lord. . . ." (1 Peter 3:1, 6.) Paul taught: "As the church is subject unto Christ, so let the wives be to their own husbands in everything." (Ephesians 5:24.) "Wives, submit yourselves unto your own husbands, as unto the Lord." (Ephesians 5:22.)

In an address to the seminary and institute of religion personnel and their wives in September 1975 President

Kimball underlined Paul's teachings with these words:

One of the most provocative and profound statements in holy writ is Paul's instruction to husbands and wives concerning their duty to each other and to family. First he commands the women:

"Wives, submit yourselves unto your own husbands, as unto the Lord." (Ephesians 5:22.) *As unto the Lord. As unto the Lord* subject to your own husbands, he says. *As unto the Lord.* Can you conceive that? Does that mean something to you as you listen to the Lord's counsel, do his will, follow his righteous precepts, serve him faithfully?

"For the husband is the head of the wife, even as Christ is the head of the church." (Ephesians 5:23.)

Can you find in all holy scriptures where the Lord Jesus Christ failed his church? Can you find any scripture where he was untrue to his people, to his neighbors, friends, or associates? Was he faithful, was he true? Could you ask anything good and worthy that he did not give? Then that is what we ask, what he asks of a husband, *every* husband, then that is the goal. Everything he asks for us to do is for our own good. Can you think of a single exception in his great life?

"Therefore as the church is subject unto Christ, so let the wives be to their own husbands in everything." (Ephesians 5:24.)

Many misconceptions, many errors are creeping into the thoughts of many human beings in our day. And we hope, that you sisters will lead the way, lead the procession of women who understand the great opportunities that may come to them, the great responsibilities. For opportunity and responsibility go hand in hand.

This is no idle jest, no facetious matter. Much is said in Paul's word: ". . . as unto the Lord." Let it sink deep into your hearts. A woman needs to have no fear of being imposed upon or of any dictatorial measures or of any improper demands when the husband is thoughtful, self-sacrificing, and worthy. Certainly no intelligent woman would hesitate to give submission to her own truly righteous husband in everything. We are sometimes shocked to see the wife take over the leadership, naming the one to pray, the place to be, the things to do.

Husbands are commanded: "love your wives, even as Christ also loved the church, and gave himself for it." (Ephesians 5:25.)

Scripture says, "Greater love hath no man than he give his life for his friend." (John 15:13.) Your wife is your friend. You should be willing to go even to the extent of giving your life. I mean *your* life for your wife if the need should appear. Would you give your life for her? Would you ask yourself: can you love your wives even as Christ also has loved the Church? Can you think of how He loved the Church; its every breath was important to Him. He gave to those people all of His energy; all of His power; all of His interests; His life, and what more could one give. He gave His life voluntarily. . . . When the husband is ready to treat his household in that manner, that means his wife and his children, not only the wife but all the family, will respond to his loving and exemplary leadership. He won't be autocratic—won't need to demand; it will come because she will want to do what is very evidently necessary.

Certainly if fathers are to be respected, they must merit respect—if they are to be loved, they must be consistent, lovable, understanding, and kind, and they must honor their priesthood. They must see themselves as fortunate trustees of precious spirit children whom God has entrusted to their care.

What great incentives the mother has to honor and build up her worthy husband in the esteem of the offspring when she knows that this contributes to the well-adjusted lives of her children! And what a great incentive the father has for rising to his tallest spiritual stature to merit the love and respect of all members of the family.

President Joseph Smith also taught that the husband's authority is respected—even if he is wrong. He forbade missionaries to influence a wife and children to embrace the gospel if the husband and father disapproved. (HC 2:263.) The following story illustrates the point:

A young lady missionary was nearly through with her mission and hadn't brought one person to the point of being baptized into the Church. So she was especially joyful when she and her companion found a sixteen-year-old girl who was very ready to be taught. This young woman was thrilled with each of the lessons they taught her. Everything was going beautifully until, during one of the last discussions, the girl's father walked in and invited the missionaries to leave immediately and never to return. He didn't want his daughter hearing all that "garbage." The daughter was in tears as she pled with him to reconsider, but he was adamant. Finally the missionaries, remembering their instructions, said, "We respect you as head of this home—so we'll abide by your decision." Then they left, feeling completely defeated.

About two weeks later the sisters were surprised by a telephone call from the girl's father. He said, "I still think it's a bunch of bunk, but my girl wants it so badly that it's all right with me for you to continue teaching her." Shortly after that the daughter received her parents' permission to be baptized, and when the missionary left to come home, the whole family, including the father, had committed to baptism.

Elder Boyd K. Packer told my son-in-law and his fellow missionaries: "If my senior companion were to tell me to 'go jump in the lake' he'd better have a towel ready." Then he explained that when a supervisor knows that you will follow him without question he becomes much more careful about what he asks you to do.

If a woman marries a man who has honestly committed himself to follow the Lord and then plays her comforting, confidence-building role properly, she needn't worry about him leading her to hell, in any definition of the word. Perhaps this is what President Kimball meant when, at the Relief Society conference in October 1975, he said: "No woman has ever been asked by the Church authorities to follow her husband into an evil pit. She is to follow him as he follows and obeys the Savior of the world, but in deciding this, she should always be fair." (*Ensign,* March 1976, p. 72.) Being fair surely entails playing well the role that the Lord has assigned to us and fully expressing our confidence that our husbands will perform beautifully.

And, back to our analogy, that role means being the wall of the home as the husband is the foundation. Consider what walls do: they shelter and comfort, they beautify (historically whenever men live alone without the woman's touch their level of culture and beauty goes way down), and they determine how high the structure will rise and how elevated the children will be. In no way are the walls of a house inferior to the foundation, but their role is different. The problem today, I believe, is that historically foundations have crumbled too many times and let walls and roof planks come tumbling down to destruction. The consequent distrust may explain why some walls today are wanting to become foundations—why many women are wanting to commit suicide as women and become men.

If we all played the foundation role we'd have no place to live but basement houses; in that situation the roof planks (children) wouldn't be raised very high. The walls have the responsibility to elevate the roof, and how close our families get to heaven depends largely on our own success in fulfilling this responsibility.

The Sacred Triangle

*I*n general conference a few years ago Elder Matthew Cowley of the Council of the Twelve told us that a really good marriage is a partnership composed of not just two, but of three individuals: the wife, the husband, and the Lord. He called this partnership the sacred triangle and repeated that all three entities were necessary for optimum happiness in the marriage. He noted that too many couples were not allowing God to play his role, "and after divorcing God, it is practically impossible for them to stay together side by side." (CR, October 1952, p. 27.)

Not only must God be included in the triangle, he must also be allowed to play his role without interference by the wife. We need to "stay on our own acreage," play the role assigned to us, and let our husbands and the Lord play theirs. God is the helper-judge, the husband is the bearer of burdens and decision maker, and the wife is the comfort-giver.

I was married for twenty years before I learned these things. I was trying to be a good wife, but I was going way beyond my stewardship and trying to put on a one-woman show, I think. I didn't mean to be overzealous, but I was.

As I finally recognized this and pondered why, I came to the shocking conclusion that my problem was a lack of faith. I didn't really believe that the Lord would play his part, that my husband would play his part, and that all I had to do was to excel as a comfort-giver. Down deep I

24

guess I didn't really believe that I could cast my burden of worry on the Lord and trust him to cause things to work out right. Proverbs 21:1 tells us, "The king's heart is in the hand of the Lord . . . he turneth it whithersoever he will." Kings of the home (husbands) who have become hard-hearted as their wives have cut away at their egos make the Lord's heart-turning job much more difficult. So, as wives, if we comfort our husbands so well that they remain tenderhearted, the Lord can turn them easily, molding them into kings of heaven.

A young father in our ward testified of this principle in action. He said he used to be afflicted with a terrible temper. He had returned home from a very frustrating day at work and started to blow up at his family. Catching himself, he asked them to leave him alone, and went out to the front lawn to be by himself. As he sat there, trying to suppress the rising anger he felt within, a sudden, unexpected calmness came over him. He was at peace and, for the first time in his life, in complete control. As he entered his front door a little child ran up to him and said, "We prayed for you, Daddy." His wife confirmed the story. She and the children had knelt in a circle and taken turns praying for the Lord to bless their husband and father. This family trusted the Lord to uphold his part of the triangle, and they were not disappointed.

Besides having faith in the Lord to play his role without meddling, we need to have faith in our husbands to hold up their end of the triangle. We need to remember that they have keys to sources of knowledge that we don't have; that the decisions they make just might be right, even if the decisions don't agree with ours. It isn't easy to remember this.

It wasn't easy for Julia. Her husband had recently graduated from college and took his family to live with his parents until he could recover financially from college expenditures. Such living arrangements, as everyone knows,

25

are generally not the happiest; they're hard on all members of the two-family household. Julia didn't like her husband's decision—told him so with enthusiasm and frequency—and still he moved her to his parents' house. What would she do? If she were living the first principle of the gospel, if she truly had faith in the Lord Jesus Christ, she had no choice but to wholeheartedly submit to her husband's authority. She would play her comforting, confidence-building role skillfully and go to the Lord frequently in mighty prayer for strength for herself and help for her husband to work things out properly.

Julia was smarter than I; she put the above formula to work. She supported her husband's decision graciously even though it looked as if he would never be brave enough to finance a home of their own. Just six weeks after this trial of her faith she came to tell me that they would be moving in a few days, not to the shack she had been willing to accept, but to her dream house. An opportunity had suddenly come to her husband to buy a brand-new house priced far below its market value, and on such easy terms that he couldn't turn it down. It is another of the many cases reported to me of how beautifully things work out when the sacred triangle is faithfully and patiently applied to a marriage.

When the Lord "turns the king's heart" around, the king feels good about himself. When the wife yanks it around, the heart shrinks and hardens.

The sacred triangle has only three parts, however, even when a couple is living with relatives. President Kimball emphasized this point in one of his conference talks. He quoted from the Bible and then continued:

"Thou shalt love thy wife with all thy heart, and shall cleave unto her and none else." (D&C 42:22.) And when the Lord says *all* thy heart, it allows for no sharing nor dividing nor depriving. And, to the woman it is paraphrased: "Thou shalt love thy husband with *all* thy heart and shall cleave unto him and none else." The words *none else*

26

eliminate everyone and everything. The spouse then becomes pre-eminent in the life of the husband or wife, and neither social life nor occupational life nor political life nor any other interest nor person nor thing shall ever take precedence over the companion spouse. We sometimes find women who absorb and hover over the children at the expense of the husband, sometimes even estranging them from him. The Lord says to them: "Thou shalt cleave unto *him* and none else."

Marriage presupposes total allegiance and total fidelity. Each spouse takes the partner with the understanding that he or she gives self totally to the spouse: all the heart, strength, loyalty, honor, and affection with all dignity. . . .

Some who marry never cut themselves loose from the apron strings of the parents. The Lord says through his prophets: "For this cause shall a man [or woman] leave his father and mother, and shall be joined unto his wife [or husband], and they *two* shall be one flesh."

Parents who hold, direct, and dictate to their married children and draw them away from their spouses are likely to regret the possible tragedy. Accordingly, when two people marry, the spouse should become the confidant, the friend, the sharer of responsibility, and they two become independent. No one should come between the husband and wife, not even parents. (CR, October 1962, pp. 58-60.)

This kind of commitment is not easy, nor is it inexpensive. It takes the best effort an individual can give, but it's worth it. A striking realization of that fact came to me in connection with a trip we once took through the Holy Land. We had spent ten wonderful days in Israel and were back in Tel Aviv awaiting our flight to Athens for another week's sightseeing, when inadvertently my husband said something that cut deeply into my feeling of well-being. It was already the low part of the trip and so I reacted rashly, reverting to my old independence. Forgetting that we were traveling on a joint passport I said, "You go on with the rest, but I'm going home as quick as I can get there; I'm catching the next plane for New York, whether you like it or not!" He didn't say much, only, "You can't; they won't let you in without me." Well, I was so shocked with the truth of his words that I was stunned into silence, and finally into meekness. I couldn't get home without him! So I kept my mouth shut, went to Greece with the rest of the group, and had a wonderful time.

Later I came to the realization that thirty years ago we took out another joint passport—one that came from the Idaho Falls Temple and is to last for eternity. In the same way, neither one of us is going to "get home" without the other. Knowing that fact makes the great expense of being a true helpmeet well worth it.

Sweetening the Lemonade

*U*nderstanding what makes a good lemonade can help a couple understand better how to keep the commandment to be as one. Lemonade is made of three ingredients: juice, sugar, and water. A good marriage also has three essential components: the man, the wife, and the Lord. The juice, the agent that decides the flavor distinction, is like the husband; the sweetening agent that "comforts" the sourness of the juice and enhances its tart delightfulness is like the wife; and the agent that provides for expansion and real refreshment, the life-giving water, is like the Lord.

Are all three ingredients necessary? Lemon juice by itself has some limited uses, but it is glorified (Let thy delight be the glory that shall come upon thy husband—see D&C 25:14) when mixed with sugar. The sweetening agent of our recipe is not distasteful by itself, but it reaches its full potential when it is enhancing a flavor. Juice and sugar mixed together are palatable, but not thirst-quenching as they are when they are mixed with water. And notice how water adapts itself to meet the need of the moment: it can be icy cold, hot, carbonated, etc. As adaptable to all of our needs is "living water" that refreshes us permanently. (John 4:10-14.)

Once the ingredients have been gathered together, the next vital step is to blend them well. It's an unpleasant potion when the juice or the sugar is so concerned with retaining its own identity that it won't realize that the whole is greater than the sum of its parts. Sugar that won't blend is in an especially precarious position; it remains on the bottom. Only as its molecules blend are they uplifted.

Wives worry about losing their identity as they become *Mrs.* John Doe. But has the sugar really lost its identity because it has blended? Its energy-giving presence is obvious—its absence would be a disaster. Sugar never needs to question its worth; we as wives never need to question our vitally important role and our great potential as we yield our distinctiveness to create a well-blended, constantly refreshing marriage—as we become "one flesh."

Blossoms on the Tree

O ne of the real threats to unity in the home is the ever-increasing allure of outside activities and their accompanying glory. Section 25 of the Doctrine and Covenants indicates that the Lord recognizes and approves of the possibilities for women to advance in areas outside the home—to a limited extent.

This revelation specifies several activities for Emma Smith that would take her attention away from her family, i.e., acting as a scribe for the translation of the Book of Mormon, compiling a hymnbook for the Church, expounding scripture and exhorting the Church, and being the elect lady.

Then, after discussing these possibilities, the Savior warns Emma, and all wives, to be meek, to beware of pride, and to "let thy soul delight in thy husband and the glory which shall come upon him." (V. 14.)

Why bother to work for glory if it will come upon our husbands instead of ourselves? The Lord explains that "except thou do this, where I am you cannot come." We can only get as close to exaltation as our husbands can take us. It's not unlike having to accept the socioeconomic status of our husbands in this life. We work for their glory in this life so that we can be glorified alongside them in eternity.

Section 25 set the pattern for the divine directives that have followed. Several of the prophets have said that women have capabilities other than homemaking that should be developed and used, provided these women truly put their family responsibilities first. Representative of these statements is this one of President David O. McKay:

> I do not know that there is any objection to women entering the fields of literature, science, art, social economy, study and progress, and all kinds of learning, or participating in any and all things which contribute to the fullness of her womanhood and increase her upbuilding influence in the world; but I do know that there are three areas or realms in which women's influence should always be felt. . . . The first is the realm of home building. Next to that is the realm of teaching, and the third, the realm of compassionate service. (*Improvement Era,* August 1965, p. 676.)

To his own daughter, Susa Young Gates (who became one of Utah's most accomplished and renowned women), Brigham Young gave this advice: "If you were to become the greatest writer . . . the most gifted and learned woman of your time, and had neglected your home and children in order to become so . . . you will find your whole life had been a failure. . . . If, in addition to your wifely and motherly duties, you can pursue one or more fields of public labor . . . all the good that you can accomplish . . . will be so much added glory to your eternal crown." (*Young Woman's Journal,* June 1894, p. 449.)

The big problem for many women, as the Lord knew it would be back in 1830 when the possibility of such was almost nil, is the worldly recognition given to those women who excel away from home, and the lack of professional status for homemakers. The Lord warned us to beware of pride, and President Joseph F. Smith gave us these words, which are good to recall when our egos sag: "Some people would rather be the blossom of a tree and be admiringly seen than to be an enduring part of the tree and live the commonplace life of the tree's existence." (*Juvenile Instructor,* December 15, 1905, p. 753.) Nothing is more lovely than beautiful, fragrant blossoms, until one remembers that in a day or two they are consigned to the trash can. Just as fleeting are the honors of men.

President Heber J. Grant's daughter had a good chance to receive worldly applause because of her great potential as a professional singer. He said that he would sooner have her sing lullabies to her own children than be the greatest singer in the world. (*Relief Society Magazine,* May 1933, p. 302.)

Seeing herself as having high professional status as a homemaker, recognizing that she and her husband are operating a laboratory where they are developing embryonic gods will make a woman much more contented to stay at home.

"She must account every other thing as beneath the domestic in importance and power. She must feel that in passing from any one or all of these she ascends when she enters or resumes the domestic life." (David O. McKay, *Relief Society Magazine,* December 1953, p. 795.)

A Good Neighbor

Although a Latter-day Saint wife's first responsibility is to her family, she is expected to extend the hand of warmth and fellowship to those around her as well. As President Joseph F. Smith said: "We feel that it is the first duty of Latter-day Saints to take care of themselves, and of their poor; and then, if we can extend it to others . . . we feel that it is our duty to do it. But first look after the members of our own household." (CR, April 1915, p. 10.)

As possessors of "refined feelings and sensitiveness" (HC 5:19), women are especially well-equipped to reach out to others. But the Prophet Joseph Smith noted that these qualities could also prove dangerous, as they sometimes cause women to be rigid and apt to do more harm than good in their efforts to reform. The following example illustrates this point:

Mahala Overton made it to Relief Society—that first Relief Society. It wasn't the first meeting of the organization by any means; it had taken several weeks of glowing reports before she had gained the courage to try it. Then for a few minutes, which seemed like a century, she fervently wished that she had stayed at home. In those days women had to be voted on in order to belong to Relief Society. Members were to be women of high moral character, and some of the members questioned whether Mahala could meet that qualification. It took several

34

minutes of lively discussion before the objections were removed and Sister Overton received an affirmative vote as a member.

The Prophet Joseph, according to Eliza R. Snow's minutes, was in attendance at this meeting, and his acrid remarks at the time make important reading to any woman who wants to be a good neighbor. He said:

> Suppose that Jesus Christ and holy angels should object to us on frivolous things, what would become of us? [The Relief Society sisters hadn't thought they were such frivolous things.]
>
> It grieves me that there is no fuller fellowship; if one member suffer all feel it; by union of feeling we obtain power with God. Christ said He came to call sinners to repentance. . . . It is the object of this society to reform persons, not to take those that are corrupt and foster them in their wickedness; but if they repent, we are bound to take them, and by kindness sanctify and cleanse them from all unrighteousness by our influence in watching over them. Then take Sister Overton, as Jesus received sinners into His bosom. Sister Overton, in the name of the Lord, I now make you free. Nothing is so much calculated to lead people to forsake sin as to take them by the hand, and watch over them with tenderness. . . .
>
> . . . The nearer we get to our heavenly Father, the more we are disposed to look with compassion on perishing souls; we feel that we want to take them upon our shoulders, and cast their sins behind our backs. My talk is intended for all this society; if you would have God have mercy on you, have mercy on one another. . . .
>
> . . . If the sisters loved the Lord, let them feed the sheep and not destroy them. . . . There should be no license for sin, but mercy should go hand in hand with reproof. (HC 5:23-24.)

President Brigham Young pointed out another way in which well-meaning neighbors might do more harm than good. He told the Relief Society members to help those in unfortunate circumstance, but "to give to the idler is as wicked as anything else. Never give anything to the idler." (JD 16:19.)

President Young didn't want anyone who was able to suffer the harmful effects of "eating the bread of charity." People should be helped to sustain themselves so that all could go to bed each night peacefully aware that they had performed their duties.

My father helped me to learn this concept when I was a young Relief Society president. I was determined to be an "angel of mercy" to the members of my ward; no one was going to be in want while I was in office. One day the bishop called me to visit a family in the ward and write up an order for food for them; the husband had lost his job, and their cupboards were bare. I was doing this service at their home when the husband walked in and said, "Thanks, but no thanks. I'll take care of my family myself."

His wife cried—she didn't know what she was going to use to put supper on the table—and I pleaded with him. "You have spent as much time picking beans at the welfare farm as any man in the ward," I reminded him. "You have earned these supplies." Still he refused help.

Shortly after this meeting my parents came to visit us, and I told them about this man and how foolish I thought he was. Then my father shocked me by upholding the man's decision, saying, "My dear, when you have robbed a man of his independence you have left him very poor indeed."

Fear of making mistakes like this should never keep us from our neighborly responsibilities, but should serve to remind us that we are in constant need of the Lord's guidance as we work to help his children. Joseph F. Smith decried the lack of neighborliness he had seen, especially in large cities where people "live so near each other that they can almost shake hands, from door to door, yet never call, nor associate together." He hoped that Saints wouldn't exhibit such exclusiveness but would demonstrate the "warmth of the gospel." (*Improvement Era,* October 1904, p. 959.)

Sharing this gospel warmth with our neighbors may help in the Church's missionary efforts by making people more receptive to the Lord's teachings. This fulfills in part our responsibilities as member missionaries, and opens the way for others to partake of the happiness we enjoy. So much can be accomplished by a woman who has acquired the skill of being a good neighbor.

Looking the Part

Much of the success achieved in spreading the gospel involves impressions. It's our responsibility to set an example for our neighbors of what the Church is all about, and one way we convey this is in our dress.

After Relief Society one day, when a group of women were discussing clothes and grooming, one said, "My husband says he can pick the Mormons out of a gathering every time." Studying the scriptures, ancient and latter-day, on the subject of fashion has made me believe that this should be the case. Mormons should surely be well-groomed, but they should also be distinctive in a crowd—they should look like Mormons. As Alma told us, even our countenances should reflect our religious ideals. (Alma 5:14.)

Much has been said by God's spokesmen on the subject of dress ever since coats of skin were made to cover the nakedness of Adam and Eve. Though fads and fashions have changed many times through the years, the principles of being properly clothed seem to remain consistent. They might fall into the following six categories:

1. Mormons should work to keep and enhance their good looks.

2. Mormons aren't expected to dress uniformly.

3. Mormons should not let fashion designers dictate their mode of dress.

4. Women should look feminine, avoiding the unisex look in dress, which Isaiah called an abomination.

5. Mormons should look like Mormons.

6. Mormons are expected to cover their nakedness.

Let's examine each of these categories and see what the prophets have said.

1. *Mormons should work to keep and enhance their good looks.*

David O. McKay said: "It is not my purpose to discourage efforts to enhance physical beauty. When given by birth, it should be nurtured in childhood, cherished in girlhood, and protected in womanhood. When not inherited it should be developed and sought after in every legitimate and heathful manner." (*Young Woman's Journal,* August 1906, p. 360.)

"And if any of you are so superstitious and ignorant as to say that this is pride," said Brigham Young, "I can say that you are not informed as to the pride which is sinful before the Lord, you are also ignorant as to the excellency of the heavens, and of the beauty which dwells in the society of the Gods. Were you to see an angel, you would see a beautiful and lovely creature." (JD 12:201.)

Spencer W. Kimball offered this advice to single women: "If you have fewer opportunities [for marriage], you need to evaluate yourself carefully. Take a careful inventory of your habits, your speech, your appearance, your weight, and your eccentricities if you have them." (*Ensign,* September 1974, p. 93.)

2. *Mormons aren't expected to dress uniformly.*

In her attempts to encourage women to retrench from frivolity in dress in the early days of Utah, Eliza R. Snow designed a uniform for all to wear: a full pantaloon outfit. It wasn't accepted by the ladies or by the prophet. President Young said that it is good to have variety. He noted that in the works of God "you see an eternal variety," and that he didn't want the people to become like the Quakers and other groups who dressed uniformly. (JD 14:17.)

3. *Mormons should not let fashion designers dictate their mode of dress.*

When full skirts were in fashion, President Young worried that the Saints were using too much precious yardage in their dresses. After the styles changed he didn't like dresses that were so tight as to show the women's forms. He stated that it manifested a weakness of mind to dress after the fashions of Babylon, and the Church members should be leaders in fashion. He blamed the mothers for the "worldly" look of their daughters. (JD 14:15-22.)

President Wilford Woodruff also complained about tight dresses. He worried that women's skirts were so tight that if a woman were trying to cross a street and a runaway team threatened to run over her she wouldn't be able to jump or run to safety. Her only recourse would be to roll like a log. (JD 18:129.)

The Saints' biggest struggle with the fashion designers came during President Joseph F. Smith's tenure. For centuries women had worn long dresses, but with the Industrial Revolution women's fashions, as well as concepts of woman's role, made a big change. Skirts were shortened to the knees, and sleeves came all the way off. President Smith enthusiastically defended the Church dress standards in a general conference:

> In my sight the present-day fashions are abominable, suggestive of evil, calculated to arouse base passion and lust, and to engender lasciviousness, in the hearts of those who follow the fashions, and of those who tolerate them. Why? Because women are imitating the very customs of a class of women who have resorted to that means to aid them to sell their souls. It is infamous, and I hope the daughters of Zion will not descend to these pernicious ways, customs and fashions, for they are demoralizing and damaging in their effect. (*Conference Report,* October 1913, p. 8.)

The "Roaring Twenties" solidified the fashion change, and the next Church president, Heber J. Grant, agreed to change Church standards to make knee-length skirts and upper-length sleeves acceptable. Following that change, and within those guidelines, the present directive to Mormon women and girls is to be modest in their dress.

> The Church has not attempted to indicate just how long women's or girls' dresses should be nor whether they should wear pant suits or other types of clothing. We have always counseled our members to be modest in their dress, maintaining such standards in connection therewith as would not be embarrassing to themselves and to their relatives, friends and associates.
>
> We have advised our people that when going to the temple they should not wear slacks or mini-skirts, nor otherwise dress immodestly. We have not, however, felt it wise or necessary to give instructions on this subject relative to attendance at our Church meetings, although we do feel that on such occasions they should have in mind that they are in the house of the Lord and should conduct themselves accordingly. (First Presidency, *New Era*, August 1971, p. 50.)

Much study has been given to the psychological effect of the clothes people wear and how one's costume really does affect one's behavior. There is much empirical data to support the theory that people's perceptions of themselves as well as other people's perceptions of them are greatly affected by the clothing worn. As the mother of eight, I have surely seen how, from the time the children were tiny, their actions have been much in line with the way they were dressed.

An incident in my own life really impressed upon me the effects of clothing on behavior. I was in a professional opera chorus giving a production of Bizet's *Carmen.* Carmen and the characters depicted by the chorus were not Mormon-type girls, and as a Mormon matron I was having a difficult time playing the part—until I put on the flamboyant costume they handed to me. With this dress I had to wear brief underwear. It was amazing to me, and to the director, how my portrayal of the role changed when I was dressed for the part. I could now shake my hips as seductively as necessary. When the show closed I was much more grateful for the promised protection given to those who fully keep Mormon dress standards.

4. *Women should look feminine.*

"The woman shall not wear that which pertaineth unto a man, neither shall a man put on a woman's garment: for all that do so are abomination unto the Lord thy God." (Deuteronomy 22:5.) This verse has been repeated by God's spokesmen in recent days. (Joseph Fielding Smith, *CR,* April 1964, p. 108.)

5. *Mormons should look like Mormons.*

Throughout history people who have wanted to be identified with one another have often tried to look alike. One example of this concept comes from the Book of Mormon. The Amlicites, having dissented from the Nephites, wanted to look different from the Nephites, so they identified themselves by putting a red mark on their foreheads. (Alma 3.) While we don't have a uniform or specific rules governing the way we will dress, we have been given some guidelines. These include modesty at all times, being well groomed and cleancut, and dressing appropriate to the occasion. There is real safety in fitting in with the rest of one's group, and Mormons, of all people on earth, should reflect in their dress the knowledge that they are truly children of God.

6. *People should cover their nakedness.*

President Joseph Fielding Smith told us that the reason that Adam and Eve were given garments was to "clothe themselves, and the Lord does not like nakedness," because the body is sacred and not for public view. (*Relief Society Magazine,* December 1966, p. 885.)

President Kimball reinforced this admonition when he said, "We pray for a generation of girls who will display their wit, their intelligence, their modest charm, their integrity, their loveliness rather than their bodies and their sexual possibilities." (*Faith Precedes the Miracle* [Deseret Book, 1975], p. 167.)

Both of these prophets join with President Young in accusing the mothers of encouraging their daughters to expose their bodies too much.

Hard as it may sometimes be, it's important for Mormons to maintain high standards of modesty and good taste in dress. Being picked out of a crowd as a Mormon should be a compliment, because it shows our willingness to set an example in all things. Mormons *should* look like Mormons.

Blessings of
Eternal Increase

Hand in hand with looking like a Mormon is acting like one, and Mormons' opinions on matters of social concern today are becoming as unpopular as opinions on dress standards have been in the past. The Saints' stand on birth control is a good example.

Pregnaphobia is a word recently coined, and after having eight children and a miscarriage in less than twelve years, I know what it means, how it feels. We were one of those fortunate couples who were always "expecting." Even breastfeeding didn't prevent conception for us. We had three of our babies while my husband was still in school, but he managed to support us and still finish his college work.

One time, after hearing from a local Church official that "people aren't supposed to reproduce like rabbits," coupled with my doctor's advice that I should give my body a much-needed rest, I went to my parents, who had a family of twelve, for reassurance. Sympathetic with the hardship on health, energy, and economics that having a baby nearly every year brings, my father told me the following story.

Mother was not well physically; her doctor consistently warned her, from the time her fourth baby was born, that she shouldn't have any more. It was the time of the big depression and my father's school teaching wages were stretched to the limit to meet family expenses. He had sup-

44

plemented his income by working at other jobs on Saturdays, but jobs were now so scarce that "Saturday only" opportunities were nearly nonexistent. They already had nine children, a very full house, so they decided that they had done their part and would refrain from bearing any more. My father told me that he went to the drugstore and bought contraceptive supplies but couldn't bring himself to use them. Then he looked me straight in the eye and said, "And you, my dear, were the *tenth* child."

Then both Mother and Father bore their testimonies to me of how their children were such a great source of satisfaction and happiness to them, of how grateful they were that all twelve of us had come along.

As always, I left their home uplifted, encouraged, and determined to "remember who I was." Now I share their testimony of the happiness that comes from being willing to bear all the children that the Lord sends. My husband and I are so happy that natural methods of birth control didn't work for us. We didn't know, in those early years of our marriage—no one knew but the Lord—that my childbearing years would soon be over, and that at age thirty-three I would suddenly become barren. God had sent our children rapidly in order to get each one here in my time span. We're so grateful that he did, though we were often dismayed at the time it was happening.

One pregnancy was especially surprising to us—we almost hadn't given the Lord an opportunity to send us Marilyn. Now we understand why she came almost without an invitation. Our eldest child had just turned four when Marilyn, our fourth baby, was born. She was very welcome long before her arrival, and was such a beautiful, good-natured cherub that she was a great joy to have. I took her for her four-month checkup on March 3, and she was declared to be in perfect health. Then, about 7 A.M. on March 5, I awoke and thought, "The baby is sleeping late today; I'll hurry and get a batch of washing done before she wakes up." Then I looked at her bed, right next to ours, and realized that she would never wake up again in mortality. "Crib death," the doctor said.

In the stillness of the night that followed I learned why my baby had been called home. I didn't see or hear anything, but it was made known to me very surely that our little Marilyn had accepted a mission call beyond the veil while she was still in premortality. She only came to receive a body, and had now gone to fill her mission.

It is comforting to know that Marilyn, and all children who die before they reach the age of accountability, will have the blessings of exaltation. President Joseph Fielding Smith said:

> The Lord will grant unto these children the privilege of all the sealing blessings which pertain to the exaltation. . . . It would be manifestly unfair to deprive a little child of the privilege of receiving all the blessings of exaltation in the world to come simply because it died in infancy. . . . Children who die in childhood will not be deprived of any blessing. When they grow, after the resurrection, to the full maturity of the spirit, they will be entitled to all the blessings which they would have been entitled to had they been privileged to tarry here and receive them. (*Doctrines of Salvation* [Bookcraft, 1955], 2:54.)

Now that I'm barren and look at others carrying their little, pink bundles, I am so grateful to realize that my arms are only temporarily empty. I still have a little, pink bundle in my future. Joseph Smith promised several worthy mothers the privilege of raising these little bodies to maturity in the resurrection. (See *HC* 4:556.) It's the only way I've found that we can raise a flesh-and-bones baby after mortality. We're so grateful that we didn't prevent the Lord from sending Marilyn before my fertility span ended.

We learned another lesson at this time that may be helpful to others. Several people told us that there are things worse than death. One of these dear friends told me how her first baby died and when her second baby came he was not healthy either. Not being able to accept the thought of being again bereaved, she said she demanded that the Lord let this child live. The Lord complied. "And now I have a very afflicted child," she said. The boy had grown to physical maturity but only had the mentality of a two-year-old. I was grateful then that the Lord hadn't given me a chance to interfere with his will. When his purposes are the cause of pain to us, he supplies the balm to ease that pain; but it takes eyes of faith to see this as the hurt comes on.

My testimony goes right along with Church policy on birth control: it is between the couple and the Lord. As with other pertinent questions on the husband-wife relationship, general guidelines have been given on whether children should be carefully spaced, but for specific direction the couple is directed to go to the Lord.

These two official statements define the guidelines:

We seriously regret that there should exist a sentiment or feeling among any members of the Church to curtail the birth of their children. We have been commanded to multiply and replenish the earth that we may have joy and rejoicing in our posterity.

Where husband and wife enjoy health and vigor and are free from impurities that would be entailed upon their posterity, it is contrary to the teachings of the Church artificially to curtail or prevent the birth of children. We believe that those who practice birth control will reap disappointment by and by.

However, we feel that men must be considerate of their wives who bear the greater responsibility not only of bearing children, but of caring for them through childhood. To this end the mother's health and strength should be conserved and the husband's consideration for his wife is his first duty, and self-control a dominant factor in all their relationships.

It is our further feeling that married couples should seek inspiration and wisdom from the Lord that they may exercise discretion in solving their marital problems, and that they may be permitted to rear their children in accordance with the teachings of the gospel. (The First Presidency, Letter to stake presidents, bishops, and mission presidents, April 14, 1969.)

In view of a recent decision of the United States Supreme Court, we feel it necessary to restate the position of the Church on abortion in order that there be no misunderstanding of our attitude.

The Church opposes abortion and counsels its members not to submit to or perform an abortion except in the rare cases where, in the opinion of competent medical counsel, the life or good health of the mother is seriously endangered or where the pregnancy was caused by rape and produces serious emotional trauma in the mother. Even then it should be done only after counseling with the local priesthood authority and after receiving divine confirmation through prayer.

Abortion must be considered one of the most revolting and sinful practices in this day, when we are witnessing the frightening evidence of permissiveness leading to sexual immorality.

Members of the Church guilty of being parties to the sin of abortion must be subjected to the disciplinary action of the councils of the Church as circumstances warrant. In dealing with this serious matter, it would be well to keep in mind the word of the Lord stated in the 59th section of the Doctrine and Covenants, verse 6, "Thou shalt not steal; neither commit adultery, nor kill, nor do anything like unto it."

As to the amenability of the sin of abortion to the laws of repentance and forgiveness, we quote the following statement made by President David O. McKay and his counselors, Stephen L Richards and J. Reuben Clark, Jr., which continues to represent the attitude and position of the Church:

"As the matter stands today, no definite statement has been made by the Lord one way or another regarding the crime of abortion. So far as is known, He has not listed it alongside the crime of the unpardonable sin and shedding of human blood. That He has not done so would suggest that it is not in that class of crime and therefore that it will be amenable to the laws of repentance and forgiveness."

This quoted statement, however, should not in any sense be construed to minimize the seriousness of this revolting sin. (The First Presidency, *Church News,* January 27, 1973, p. 7.)

President Joseph Fielding Smith made another statement about curtailing the birth of children that is so important that it needs to be included here, because the people who curtail the births of children here may very well be "shutting themselves off from the eternal blessing of increase."

Now I wish to ask a question: How will a young married couple feel when they come to the judgment and then discover that there were certain spirits assigned to them and they refused to have them? Moreover, what will be their punishment when they discover that they have failed to keep a solemn covenant and spirits awaiting this mortal life were forced to come elsewhere when they were assigned to this particular couple. . . .

I regret that so many young couples are thinking today more of successful contraceptives than of having a posterity. They will have to answer for their sin when the proper time comes and actually may be denied the glorious celestial kingdom. (*Improvement Era,* December 1965, p. 1107.)

This divine denial of progeny, as a result of purposeful curtailment by a couple, may very well happen in mortality as well. A student told me of how her sister and brother-in-law had been in their first year of college when they married, so they decided to wait until they both had their academic degrees before taking on the burden of parenthood. The degrees were awarded and the babies were then invited—but none came. Finally they went to a General Authority for a blessing to help them have children. He was eager to help and started to give the blessing; then he stopped. It had been made known to him that there had been spirits scheduled to come to this couple, but in refusing to accept them, these people had forfeited their right to be parents. "You can only decide when you won't have children. The Lord decides when you will have children." (Hartman Rector, Jr., Brigham Young University, *Daily Universe,* January 9, 1973.)

God's spokesmen, the prophets, have continually told us not to curtail child-bearing because of economic stress. President David O. McKay noted that many people honestly limit the number of children they have for fear of not being able to clothe and educate them properly. Then he observed that "in nearly all such cases, the two or three children are not better provided for than two or three times that number would be." (*Relief Society Magazine,* July 1916, p. 366.) He warned that procrastinating the bringing of children into the homes of young couples is very risky to marital happiness. (*Church News,* June 11, 1952, p. 3.)

Bishop Marvin O. Ashton, a former member of the Presiding Bishopric, stressed this point with one of his delightful stories.

Down in one of the southern states there had been a bad train wreck. For some reason the details of it had not been received. The engineer pulling his regular load of cars, going on the same track and to the point reported to be the scene of the accident, was instructed to get details and report back.

Up the line fifty or more miles the train with instructions came to the spot of the trouble. There at the side of the track and sprawled on its side lay the steam monster. Just back of it but dismembered from it was the coal car, the only responsibility of our wrecked giant. Just as luck would have it, both the engineer and the fireman of the unfortunate engine had made a successful leap to safety as the locomotive left the track. The two engineers met—the one carrying his regular load of ten to fifteen cars and the unfortunate fellow who must explain things to the management of the railroad.

"Bill, what on earth was the matter?" His fellow engineer had only one answer, "Tom, I guess I was running light." Yes, he had come up the line with full steam on, sixty miles an hour, making the curves at that rate, pulling only a coal car. He was running light. . . .

Children would save many a family wreck if they would be invited to ride. . . .

Members of this Church: Many of the wrecks of life, wrecks that can't be repaired and set up on the track again, are caused because they who suffer are running light. Let us thank God that we have a load to carry. If we have, we'll take those curves better. (*To Whom It May Concern* [Bookcraft, 1956], pp. 205-6, 8.)

"They Two Shall Be One Flesh"

nother area in which the gulf between Church and world views is growing ever wider concerns premarital sex. Widespread acceptance of sex before marriage as being acceptable, even desirable, makes it increasingly difficult to help young people realize the importance of chastity.

A real dilemma crops up because sexual union is such an important part of being "one flesh" *after* the marriage ceremony. Several Mormon marriage counselors identify sexual incompatibility as the biggest problem in many Mormon marriages. One BYU Family Relationships teacher theorizes that unless we're very careful, we build this incompatibility into our culture in our effort to keep our young people chaste.

Certainly the importance of chastity cannot be overlooked, but the challenge comes in looking for a way to teach premarital sexual abstinence without hampering a couple's ability to become one after they are properly married.

One friend of mine has handled this challenge in a way that seems to be effective. She teaches her seminary students to consider themselves to be sexually fasting before marriage. Fasting is a concept that they can easily identify with, and though they recognize it as a difficult discipline, they can endure it because they look forward to the eventual feasting. Applying this concept to sexual behavior helps young people remain chaste without growing up with the damaging feeling that sexual feasting is inherently wrong.

Youngsters used to first-of-the-month fasting readily agree that it's very wrong, while fasting, to nibble. Nibbling is wrong because it causes one to feel guilty, lowering precious self-esteem. Also, nibbling usually leads to full participation, which was not originally intended. Almost before they are aware of it they are saying, "I can't believe I ate the whole thing." During a fast-Saturday night it isn't wrong to acknowledge that one is hungry, unless one dwells on the subject. Looking at pictures of tempting dishes is the worst thing to do at this time; viewing pornography has the same devastating effect on sexual fasts. The best plan, when one is hungry, is to get the mind filled with other thoughts and activities.

The fast, in both cases, is legally ended by a sacred Church ceremony. Then, upon returning from the church and finding the table laden with the feast, there is no reason for not partaking of it joyously. Guilt feelings have no place here. However, we don't just "dig in" as barbarians would. As always, good manners are the rule, and any action that offends the sensitivities of the other participants would most certainly be out of place. Overindulgence would, of course, also bring discomfort.

One other action must not be overlooked at this time. Before partaking, the family offers thanks to the Creator of the feast and asks his blessing upon it. Then, as with the creator of any good feast, He is glad to see the participants joyfully receive his offering. As the third member of the marriage partnership, he even offers very real help in this, as in all other facets of married life. Elder Parley P. Pratt of the Council of the Twelve told us that the gift of the Holy Spirit "increases, enlarges, expands, and purifies all the natural passions and affections and adapts them, by the gift of wisdom, to their lawful use. It inspires, develops, cultivates, and matures all the fine-toned sympathies, joys, tastes, kindred feelings, and affections of our nature." (*Key to the Science of Theology* [Deseret Book, 1978 ed.], p. 61.)

After reading Elder Pratt's autobiography I concluded that he knew this from his own experience. He married his childhood sweetheart, Thankful Halsey, before he joined the Church. Thankful must have loved him very much to answer "yes" after hearing him tell her that if she could be "this and this and this" he would deem her worthy to be his wife.

Early in their married life the Pratts heard and embraced the gospel; then Thankful was "called home." Parley married again after Thankful's death, and the letters he wrote to his second wife, while he was away on his many missions, show what a very romantic man the Holy Spirit had helped him to become.

Elder Pratt hasn't been the only prophet to tell us of God's involvement in married love and sexual compatibility. Elder Mark E. Petersen has told us: "God made sex, and He pronounced it good, and in the case of human kind, He pronounced it *very* good. Sex was sacred. It was holy. Actually, it was divine. And therefore He pronounced it *very* good. Sex is so sacred, so divine, that when it is used in its proper way, those who participate become joint creators with God. . . . It is a spark of Deity in every one of us." ("Chastity" [BYU Press, 1953], pp. 11-12.)

Elder Bruce R. McConkie has said, "I am firmly convinced that it is possible for a man or a woman to love his or her companion more abundantly in . . . marriage than it is ever possible to love such an individual outside this order of marriage, because we are entitled to have, and we do have, all of the normal and wholesome affection that does and should exist between the sexes and then in addition to that we can have in our family unit the sanctifying influence of the love of Christ." (*BYU Speeches of the Year*, November 15, 1955, p. 2.)

"Sexual union is lawful in wedlock," said President Joseph F. Smith, "and if participated in with right intent is honorable and sanctifying." (*Gospel Doctrine*, p. 309.)

Finally, President Joseph Fielding Smith said that "marriage is a principle that, when entered into, presents more challenges and blessings than any other. It should be lived in the spirit of patience and love, even that greater love which comes through the power of the Holy Spirit." (*Improvement Era*, September 1970, p. 3.)

Even people not yet blessed with the gift of the Holy Ghost bear testimony of how turning to God has brought sexual fulfillment to their marriages. According to a recent national survey, the women who identified themselves as being sexually fulfilled were invariably the women who identified themselves as being religious, and vice versa. The reporter concluded that "sex and religion must be a marriage made in heaven." (*Redbook*, April 1976, p. 103.)

The following poem expresses well the position of the Church on this issue:

> If God is love,
> The source,
> The spring,
> Should not the lover
> Pilgrimage there—
> Reverently
> Seeking supply?—
> That the cup he gives
> Will not be dry.
> —Carol Lynn Pearson*

Because of the sacred nature of sexual union, little has been said by God's spokesmen to answer questions that arise. The official position of the Church, as one temple

---

*Carol Lynn Pearson, *The Search* (Provo, Utah: Trilogy Arts, 1970), p. 7. Used by permission of the author.

president told me he had been instructed to tell questioners, is, "It's between the couple and the Lord." Some guidelines have been published, however, to help with general questions. Much has been said, for example, as to the purpose of sexual union:

"Marriage is for a higher purpose than for mere physical gratification. It has as its divine purpose the rearing of a family. Only by consummating this ideal can true and lasting happiness come." (David O. McKay, *Man May Know For Himself* [Deseret Book, 1967], p. 220.)

"God made sex, but not for entertainment. It was provided for a divinely appointed act of creation in which we, to this extent, become co-creators with him." (Mark E. Petersen, *Improvement Era*, June 1969, p. 78.)

"Seeking the pleasures of conjugality without a willingness to assume the responsibilities of rearing a family is one of the onslaughts that now batter at the structure of the American home." (David O. McKay, *Improvement Era*, June, 1969, p. 2.)

Procreation is not the only purpose of sex in marriage, however. Parley P. Pratt told us that it is "also for mutual affection, . . . for mutual comfort and assistance in this world of sorrow." (*Key to the Science of Theology*, 1978 ed., p. 105.) President McKay urged married people to be driven by their God-given, heaven-bestowed passions to help keep courtship paramount in their lives. (*Improvement Era*, November 1970, p. 8.)

Very few guidelines have been given about methodology—what actions are appropriate and what aren't. If gospel light is turned on in the bedroom, if the sacred triangle is used there, if a couple consider their bedroom as their "holy-of-holies" and enter in it to give all the joy they can, little published instruction would be asked. The problem is that we're being pulled from the iron rod by two poles. On the one extreme we have the negative but very powerful Victorian tradition; at the other is the prevailing philosophy of "anything goes." Victorian tradition that looks at joyous sexual union of spouses with a frowning face is not Mormon doctrine.

Tradition, not Mormon doctrine, labels Eve as the lustful mother of all sin.

Tradition, not Mormon doctrine, labels women as base creatures put here only for the purpose of replenishing the earth.

Tradition, not Mormon doctrine, labels the body as a shameful thing not to be looked upon by one's spouse.

Tradition, not Mormon doctrine, says that it is a sin to caress one's spouse.

Tradition, not Mormon doctrine, fosters the concept that there should be no pleasure in sexual intercourse, that it is a duty only, a distasteful duty that must be done only to beget children.

The Church of Jesus Christ of Latter-day Saints has been fighting the piety of sectarianism ever since the days of Joseph Smith, but these traditions are deeply rooted and not easily dispelled. On the other hand, the Church is also fighting the concept that sensual pleasure is of prime importance. Mere pleasure is not good enough, as President McKay said:

"Let us in life distinguish between the joy that the Prophet Lehi had in mind when he said 'men are, that they might have joy,' and the pleasure that the world is seeking by indulging in appetites and pastimes, vainly hoping to find happiness. Happiness springs from within. . . . Pleasure is not the purpose of man's existence. Joy is." (*Gospel Ideals* [Deseret News Press, 1953], pp. 491-92.)

Satan offers a cheap counterfeit to every one of the Lord's gifts to man, and sex is no exception. The Lord has told us that our bodies are his temples; Satan would have us see them as taverns. This temple-versus-tavern attitude makes a great difference in the appropriateness of sexual actions. A kiss can be uplifting or degrading depending upon the attitude. Temples of stone are made for *full* usage, with reverence, and only those who qualify for temple recommends are allowed this usage. People receiving temple recommends have demonstrated their willingness and ability to accept the responsibility that such usage incurs. Only my husband holds the recommend (the marriage license) to use my temple, and he has covenanted to accept the responsibility of caring for that temple.

President J. Reuben Clark gave us a poem that tells us how he reverenced his wife's temple:

How fair is the daughter of Zion,
Whose body is unsullied.
How serene is her brow,
That houses the pure mind.

How clear is her eye shining with the light of truth,
How beautiful are her cheeks unblushed with shame.
How sweet are her lips untasting, untasting of forbidden
    fruits.
How lovely are her arms shaped for the nurturing of
    motherhood.

How sacred are her breasts
Life fountains for the babes born of her flesh.
How holy is her body
For the fashioning of her offspring, begot under the
    covenant.

How angel-like is her mind,
The dwelling place of righteousness,
How priceless is her soul
Daughter of God, glorified for the eternities.*

---

*"Hymn to the Daughters of Zion," song published by the Young Women's Mutual Improvement Association, 1953.

Careless use of buildings belongs to tavern-users, not temple-users. Using the temple as if it were a tavern, thus degrading it, is exploitation, and as President Kimball has told us, "To love is to give, not to take. To love is to serve, not to exploit." In this same speech President Kimball said, "If sex relations merely become a release or a technique . . . then sex returns to the compulsive animal level." ("Love versus Lust," address to BYU student body, January 5, 1965.) He remarked another time that "even marriage does not make proper certain extremes in sexual indulgence." (*The Miracle of Forgiveness* [Bookcraft, 1969], p. 73.)

Some techniques of sexual skill have been talked about a great deal by God's spokesmen. President David O. McKay summed it up with two words: courtesy and kindness. He constantly urged young couples to think of the marriage ceremony as the beginning of courtship—eternal courtship—not as the end of such. His counselor, President Hugh B. Brown, gave us this advice:

> In the marriage relationship, if love is to be kept alive and growing, it must be expressed in kindly words and thoughtful actions. Where either party takes for granted that the other knows he is loved and never tells him of it, much of the color and beauty of life will fade and what should be zestful, joy-giving companionship degenerates into lackluster, humdrum existence. The marriage will not go on the rocks if each lover continues to feel the security and warmth of hearing repeatedly, "I love you." . . .
>
> Daily investments in mutual compliments pay wonderful dividends in family solidarity, understanding and success. There is no woman but who likes to have her husband tell her he loves her, wishes to be with her, how to him she is the best-dressed woman in town, how he likes her hairdo and even her kitchen apron. Complimenting her on her appearance, her cooking, and housekeeping will prove to be a wonderful tonic to her sometimes wilting spirit. Weary men too may be revived by a word of praise, confidence, and love. "I married the best man in the world" is music to any husband's soul—and it may sweeten his tongue and soothe a temper, worn thin in the day's grind. (*You and Your Marriage* [Bookcraft, 1960], pp. 97-98.)

Another choice piece of advice, especially for wives, comes from Elder A. Theodore Tuttle:

Wives, you are supposed to court your husbands as well. We attended a stake conference recently where, during the lunch period, the good wife of the stake president hovered around and saw that we had all that we could eat. When the dessert came, she said, "Well, brethren, I hope that you all like huckleberry pie (Why did she have huckleberry pie?), because it is my husband's favorite." So we all had to eat a great big piece of huckleberry pie, because it was *her husband's* favorite. You know, he will never leave her! Girls, when you get a husband, you are supposed to spoil him and pamper him and love him. ("Becoming Goodly Parents," *BYU Speeches of the Year,* December 12, 1967, p. 9.)

This instruction on how to thoroughly enjoy the feast is not new; this concluding quotation was given in the early days of the Church by President George Q. Cannon:

I was very much delighted with some remarks President John Taylor made on this subject. He told the husbands to court their wives over again, to cultivate the feeling they had when they started out in life, when they were everything to each other, and when they could not do enough for each other. That is a feeling that should be cultivated. Men should never treat their wives with disrespect. They should manifest a feeling of love for them, and more especially when they become advanced in years. There is nothing that will excite love in a man's heart so much as to see a wife willing, even in her advanced years, to sacrifice her own comfort for his sake as she was when they were first married; and I am sure that it must have the same effect upon a woman . . . to have the husband tender and kind and loving, not forgetting her good qualities, nor what she has done. When a woman sees a husband manifest that feeling towards her, she in return will manifest her kindness and love for his thoughtful attentions. (JD 24:226.)

Principles
of Motherhood

*E*ver since God commanded Adam and Eve to multiply and replenish the earth, parents have been grappling with the challenges of raising children unto the Lord. In these latter days the pitfalls are numerous, and there is a great need for wise parental guidance and strong family ties. But the role of parent is often so confusing: how can a person ever know just how to play her part effectively enough that her children will be independent without being rebellious, strong without being stubborn, brave without being careless? Perhaps the following analogy can help.

The body is much like an automobile. Both are vehicles designed to transport us along the road of progression. Both have power enough to be a blessing or a curse; they are instruments capable of greatly helping us or destroying us. Both need to be brought into subjection, to be controlled and carefully guided to take us safely to our desired destination. This analogy puts parents in the same role as driver trainers, and looking at that role helps us more easily understand how to play the role of parental disciplinarians.

What is the driver trainer's aim? It isn't to drive the student's vehicle for him, but to teach him to drive it well himself. Parents must bend every effort to training their children to make proper decisions for their own lives—not to live their lives for them. Just as the driver trainer will not always be in the car, neither will the parent always be by the child's side, nor should he be. In either case the supervisor's task is to help the student perform well on his own.

The driver trainer has several tools to use. First, he teaches by his example before the student takes the car out on the road. Parents have an eight-year period before Satan has power over their young ones, which they should use to give this preliminary training.

Second, the driver trainer has a brake on his side of the car that he can use to halt the vehicle in cases of absolute necessity, such as prevention of a collision. Parents also have this braking prerogative, and they have been divinely directed to exercise it. King Benjamin said: "Ye will not suffer your children that they . . . transgress the laws of God, and fight and quarrel one with another, and serve the devil." (Mosiah 4:14.)

President Joseph F. Smith warned parents against failing to check their children in wrongdoing, for fear of offending them. (*Gospel Doctrine,* p. 286.) President John Taylor told parents not to allow their children to mix with any society of their choosing at all hours where they could be exposed to the wiles of the seducer and the corrupt. (*Millennial Star* 47:716.) And Alma *commanded* his son Corianton to give heed to his brothers' counsel and to refrain from iniquities. (Alma 39:10-12.)

These representative instructions, taken from different time periods, are to show permissive parents that God does expect some use of the parental brake. There are many facets to this braking, such as rebuking, but taking over the steering wheel and using force is not one of them. Because of the principle of free agency the child still makes the final decision, and that decision shouldn't be dictated forcefully by the parents.

Brigham Young said the following about parental discipline:

I will here say to parents, that kind words and loving actions toward children, will subdue their uneducated natures a great deal better than the rod, or, in other words, than physical punishment. Although it is written that, "The rod and reproof give wisdom; but a child left to himself bringeth his mother to shame," and, "he that spareth the rod hateth his son; but he that loveth him chasteneth him betimes," these quotations refer to wise and prudent corrections. Children who have lived in the sunbeams of parental kindness and affection, when made aware of a parent's displeasure, and receive a kind reproof from parental lips, are more thoroughly chastened, than by any physical punishment that could be applied to their persons. . . . The rod of a parent's mouth, when used in correction of a beloved child, is more potent in its effects, than the rod which is used on the fool's back. . . .

Kind looks, kind actions, kind words, and a lovely, holy deportment towards them, will bind our children to us with bands that cannot easily be broken; while abuse and unkindness will drive them from us, and break asunder every holy tie, that should bind them to us, and to the everlasting covenant in which we are all embraced. If my family, and my brethren and sisters, will not be obedient to me on the basis of kindness, and a commendable life before all men, and before the heavens, then farewell to all influence. Earthly kings and potentates obtain influence and power by terrorism and maintain it by the same means. Had I to obtain power and influence in that way, I should never possess it in this world or the next. (JD 10:361.)

The necessity of rebuking is mentioned in the scriptures a number of times, but we're told that it is important that this rebuking be done in such a way as to uplift and not degrade. Section 95 of the Doctrine and Covenants gives a good example of how the Lord uses this tool when he rebukes the Saints for being too slow to keep his commandment to build the Kirtland Temple, regardless of their poverty. His rebuke in this section gives three important points that parents should use as a pattern for their own disciplinary actions.

"Verily, thus saith the Lord unto you whom I love [1], and whom I love I also chasten [2] that their sins may be forgiven [3], for with the chastisement I prepare a way for their deliverance." (V. 1.) To me, this says that a good parent won't let a child continue on a path that leads to unhappiness without trying to turn him back to the

62

straight and narrow. It is a hallmark of love to chasten, and the rebuke provides a way to make atonement so that sins can be forgiven and done with, not left hanging over the child's head ad infinitum. The rebuke may be given in such a way that the atonement leaves the child's self-esteem on a high plane.

Another very important facet of proper rebuking was given in section 121 of the Doctrine and Covenants. It tells us to rebuke as directed by the Holy Ghost (eliminating tendencies to take action simply as a release of parental emotion) and to be very sure to follow the rebuke with an increased show of love. (V. 43.) Note how the Lord always leaves the self-concept on a high plane: "child of God," "man a little lower than the angels," etc. He always makes it clear that he hates the sin but loves the sinner. The constancy of his love is not threatened in his rebuking. Note also how every scriptural warning is followed by a method of deliverance.

Parents must not be so careful in their rebuking and discipline, however, that they overindulge their children. A driver trainer doesn't buy gas for his student's vehicle every time the tank is empty. This would rob his pupil of the ability to properly appreciate the gift.

My sister found this out one Christmas morning. Her living room would make one wonder if Santa Claus had emptied his whole pack there. And much of the load was for their youngest child, an adorable four-year-old. Quickly he went from one enchanting toy to another until, having looked over each one, he said, "Is that all?" Along with his parents, I was aghast, and thought that he gave a classic example of a warning that President Joseph F. Smith gave us. President Smith remarked that it is actually a cruelty to give a child everything he asks for; that children who have everything they want when they want it are most unfortunate because their capacity to enjoy has been greatly weakened by not having to wait. Parents should imitate

God's way of giving. "And what is God's way?" President Smith asks. "Everywhere in nature we are taught the lessons of patience and waiting." (*Juvenile Instructor*, July 1903, p. 400.)

God allows us to want things a long time before we get them, because the wanting of them for a length of time makes them all the more precious when they come. The seed time and harvest cycle teach one to wait: "Nature resists us and keeps admonishing us to wait, indeed we are compelled to wait." (Ibid.)

"There may be a hundred times more pleasure in a dollar piece for one child than another," President Smith said, adding that money a child works for has a value upon his life and "an actual purchasing power greatly in excess of the money that has been given to him." (Ibid., p. 401.)

Whether the following story actually happened I don't know, but the principle it illustrates is true.

A wealthy businessman wanted to retire and give his business to his son, but an unwise mother had spoiled the boy by granting his every wish. So, for a "crash training" program the father told his son that as soon as he had earned $1,000 on his own the business would be his.

Following her usual pattern the mother gave her son the money. He took it to the father and said that he had earned it. The father immediately threw it into the fireplace and watched it burn up. All the boy said was, "What did you do a dumb thing like that for?"

Then the mother reasoned that they hadn't waited long enough to make the earning of that much money plausible. So, after a couple of months this time, she handed her son another $1,000 and told him to tell his father that he had earned it. The young man complied and again the father threw the money into the fireplace and watched it burn.

Realizing that he wasn't going to fool his father, the son actually got a job and finally had the $1,000 earned. Again he took the money to his father and told him that he had earned it. The father noticed other evidences that the boy really had earned this money, but he repeated his same action. Into the fireplace went the $1,000—but this time the boy went after it and saved it from being destroyed, whereupon the father said, "Yes, that money you earned. Welcome to my business."

God has given the child two trainers to help him learn to get the best use of his vehicle. These trainers are his parents, and God has given them specific assignments. The mother is to take the first shift as the major trainer, and then the father should take over in the principal position. President Brigham Young taught: "The teachings and examples of our mothers have formed, to a great extent, our characters and directed our lives. This is their right, when they act by the power of the Priesthood, to direct the child until it is of a proper age, and then hand it over to the husband and father." (JD 9:38.)

President Young warned mothers that if this early education was neglected, the sins would not be required at the hands of the father. "Lay it to heart, ye mothers," he said, "for it will unavoidably be so. The duty of the mother is to watch over the children, and give them their early education." Then he asked the fathers to assume the major responsibilities of child training when the child became old enough to labor with them in the field. (JD 1:67.)

How old is a child when he can help his father on a farm? Apparently the father moves into the front seat as driver trainer at this point, which seems to coincide with the age of accountability.

Behavioral scientists are also discovering the importance of the father being the dominant parent for the maturing child. Some surveys show that teenage problems of promiscuity, homosexuality, drug abuse, and others are often traceable to fathers who are either unacceptable models or are absent from the home too much during a child's maturing years.

65

The question frequently arises as to what happens to a child whose father has passed away. Many authoritative statements assure us that a man's prime responsiblity in this life and the next is patriarchal. A man doesn't abandon his family just because his work is on the other side of the veil.

My own brother's family was promised, at his funeral, that "he will be with you at family home evening." They have known in the three years since his death that he has been with them. More recently than that, Elder Marion D. Hanks told the wife and young children of a deceased man that their husband and father would be close by, just as he knows that his deceased father helped to raise him. President Brigham Young said that the spirit world occupies the same area we do, and our departed loved ones see and hear us as we could see them if the veils were taken from our eyes. (JD 3:368-69.)

How old is a child before he begins learning, acquiring the knowledge that will carry him through this life? Child-development students are discovering that this process begins very early in life, but God's spokesmen have been telling the world this for over a hundred years. Brigham Young said that a child's mortal education begins before birth. He told the fathers to never cease to pray that their wives might enjoy the blessing of the Holy Ghost resting with them "that their infants may be endowed with the Holy Ghost, from their mother's womb." (JD 1:69.) Then he said: "It has been hinted that education commences with the dawn of knowledge upon the mental faculties of the child, and continues with it till death. But I will trace it back a little further still, and say that education commences with the mother and child in connection." (Ibid.) When is that connection made? President Young answered, "The spirit from the eternal worlds enters the tabernacle at the time of what is termed quickening, and forgets all it formerly knew." (JD 6:333.)

President Wilford Woodruff also told us that the education of the child begins when the spirit life from God enters into the tabernacle. The condition of the mother at that time, he warned, will affect the fruit of her womb, as her influence, teachings, and example continue to be felt throughout the child's life into eternity. (*Millennial Star* 51:593.)

Brigham Young wished that mothers could understand the importance of their children's very early impressions, for "what they imbibe from their mothers in infancy, is the most lasting upon the mind through life." (JD 1:67.) And President David O. McKay said several times that control of the child must be gained very early, during the first five years of his life. (*Relief Society Magazine,* December 1953, pp. 792-93.)

President Harold B. Lee added this insight: "Great things are required of fathers and mothers before Satan has power to tempt little children. What are the great things? Have you ever thought of that? Before Satan has a chance to lay hold on a little child, it is the responsibility of the parents to lay a solid foundation by teaching Latter-day Saint standards by example and by precept. In other words, to you and to the sisters over whom you preside, it means the making of a career of motherhood. Let nothing supercede that career." (*Relief Society Magazine,* January 1967, p. 9.)

Realizing the great importance of early training makes it much easier, in this day of so many attractive alternatives, to see that nothing is important enough to cause a mother to miss her shift in the front seat as driver trainer. The First Presidency of the Church under Heber J. Grant said:

This divine service of motherhood can be rendered only by mothers. It may not be passed to others. Nurses cannot do it; public nurseries cannot do it; hired help cannot do it—only mother, aided as much as may be by the loving hands of father, brothers, and sisters, can give the full needed measure of watchful care.

The mother who entrusts her child to the care of others, that she may do non-motherly work, whether for gold, for fame, or for civic service, should remember that "a child left to himself bringeth his mother to shame." (Proverbs 29:15.) In our day the Lord has said that unless parents teach their children the doctrines of the Church "the sin be upon the heads of the parents." (D&C 68:25.)

Motherhood is near to divinity. It is the highest, holiest service to be assumed by mankind. It places her who honors its holy calling and service next to the angels. (*CR*, October 1942, pp. 12-13.)

Even Church callings are not important enough to take a mother away from her family when it needs her. President Joseph Fielding Smith made this clear when he said, "We don't want our sisters, because of responsibilities given to them in the organizations of the Church, to neglect their families." (*Relief Society Magazine*, December 1966, p. 887.) President Harold B. Lee concurred, stating that it is a big mistake for both husband and wife to have Church assignments that take them away from the home at the same time and leave children there without them. (*Relief Society Magazine*, January 1967, p. 11.)

In our inflation-wracked society, one of the great temptations that lures mothers out of the home is the chance to bring more money, money that may be sorely needed, into the home. This was a big temptation for me when our eldest son left for his mission. We didn't have enough money to care for the needs of our big family and support his mission as well—at least, it seemed impossible.

Our youngest child was in grade school at this time, so I thought that I should get a job away from home. My husband didn't like the idea and said that the only reason I should do so would be if I couldn't be happy in staying home. Then he left the decision up to me. I prayed about it for weeks, and interviewed for several job possibilities.

No answer came to my prayers until one day when I heard an official of the juvenile court give a lecture. In answer to one woman's question about working mothers he said, "You'll lose far more than you will gain." It was impressed upon my mind, as I heard those words, that this was the answer to my prayers. The problem was that by now several tempting jobs had been offered to me, and we still had great need for more income. With eyes of faith, because both of the other members of our sacred triangle were telling me that I should stay at home, I turned down these jobs.

In a short while my husband received two unexpected promotions at his office and the added income these brought came to the exact amount I had turned down to stay home. The money crisis was over.

I'm so thankful that I don't have the guilt feelings that would have come had I willfully gone against divine counsel and divided my interests while my children were maturing. Now I can go to the Lord with a clear conscience and remind him that my husband and I have consistently put our family first. Of course, I was less than what a mother ought to be—I made plenty of mistakes—but I was always trying.

One of our sons was well on the way to wrecking his vehicle forever, but because the Lord knows we did our best, he has worked miracles in our son's behalf. He may be bruised and scarred, but he's determined to find his way to exaltation.

Because of the Savior's wonderful atonement, wrecks can be repaired. The important thing for parents to remember, in such an event, is to never, never give up, and to keep God's commandments in their own lives. The following are a few statements from the prophets that give substance to the allegation that, even though the devil may win a battle, those who follow the Lord's battle plan will win the war. Satan only has power to bruise our heels. Priesthood power will crush his ugly head.

Parents—you who continue to live the life of true Christians, and are filled with faith, virtue, and good works, I promise you, in the name of Israel's God, that you will have your children, and no power can rob you of them. . . . If they go to hell, you will have the privilege of dragging them from there, if you are faithful. (Brigham Young, JD 7:336.)

The first I would say to mothers, don't give up on the boy or girl in that insufferable state of super-egotism through which some teen-agers go. I plead with you for those boys and those girls. Don't give up on the boy or girl in that impossible stage of independence and disregard of family discipline. Don't give up on him or her when they show a shocking display of irresponsibility. The know it all, self-sufficient, want-nothing-of-counsel, which to him is just a preachment of an old-timer who has lost step with youth. . . .

We have a missionary grandson in the North British Mission. He hadn't been there very long until he wrote back an interesting letter in which he said the advice of his parents now comes back to him with great force. It is like a book on a shelf that has been there for nineteen years and he has just begun to take it down and start to read it for the first time. That is your son and your daughter. You may think they are not listening, but one time yours may be the book that they will take down and read again when they need it most. (Harold B. Lee, *Relief Society Magazine,* January 1968, p. 9.)

There is no guarantee, of course, that righteous parents will succeed always in holding their children, and certainly they may lose them if they do not do all in their power. The children have their free agency.

But if we as parents fail to influence our families and set them on the "strait and narrow way," then certainly the waves, the winds of temptation and evil will carry the posterity away from the path. . . . What we do know is that righteous parents who strive to develop wholesome influences for their children will be held blameless at the last day, and that they will succeed in saving most of their children, if not all. (Spencer W. Kimball, *Ensign,* November 1974, p. 111.)

A happy mother once told me how this principle of patience worked on her son, who had just received his mission call. In his early teens the boy had rebelled against Church standards and had gone far away from the straight and narrow path. No disciplinary methods had worked until his parents decided to try giving only positive reinforcement.

The mother tried to write down all the boy's good qualities but could only come up with two: his kindness to little children and his habit of promptness. The parents accentuated those and refrained from criticizing in other areas, and soon more virtues found their way on to the list. Rejoicing when the list boasted ten positive qualities, they kept praising him for these. "And today," his mother said, "he's worthy to go on a mission." Even though we may lose battles, we can still win the war.

In my living room sits a beautiful arrangement of dried flowers from a young couple who won their war. A few years ago, before their marriage, these people both had spiritual wrecks. The young man had a series of them that landed him in prison for a twelve-year period. It took time, lots more of it than they had anticipated, but today these two and their little children are as sweet and beautiful as any members of the Church. We had the privilege of witnessing the temple sealing of this lovely family.

Wrecks can be repaired. But they're terribly expensive, and cost an awfully lot of time and pain. Every effort should be made to prevent them.

Wreck-prevention is basically the mother's job, not only as a part of her own role, but because the father's effectiveness in his role is greatly dependent upon her. Elder Erastus Snow asked the Saints to show him a child who dishonors his father's name and he would show them "a woman that dishonours her husband and shows him disrespect, from which the children take their example." (JD 5:291.)

Brigham Young confirmed this concept by telling mothers that the success of the father's teaching was dependent upon the mother's having taught the child properly to revere the counsels of his father. He promised that if that preparation hasn't been made "it will be hard indeed for the father ever to control them." (JD 1:68.)

Mothers, it depends on us, so: "Let us, then, be determined not to listen to those who would turn us aside from a work which even angels might covet." (M. E. Scoles, *Millennial Star* 50:68.)

Index

73